A *Doones*

G. B

Dressed For Failure, I See

Selected Cartoons from
YOU GIVE GREAT MEETING, SID
Volume 1

FAWCETT CREST • NEW YORK

A Fawcett Crest Book
Published by Ballantine Books
Copyright © 1982, 1983 by G.B. Trudeau

Library of Congress Catalog Card Number: 83-80662

ISBN 0-449-20199-6

This edition published by arrangement with Holt, Rinehart and
Winston

The cartoons in this book have appeared in newspapers in the
United States and abroad under the auspices of Universal Press
Syndicate.

Manufactured in the United States of America

First Ballantine Books Edition: September 1984

10 9 8 7 6 5 4 3 2 1

Dressed For Failure, I See

IT IS A SPECIAL HONOR FOR ME TO SPEAK HERE ON BEHALF OF A VALUED MEMBER OF MY CABINET. RAY'S A FIGHTER, AND I'M PROUD OF THE WAY HE HAS DEVOTED THE LAST TWO YEARS TO DEFENDING HIMSELF!

THANK GOODNESS WE DON'T LIVE IN BRITAIN, WHERE EVEN THE **APPEARANCE** OF IMPROPRIETY OFTEN LEADS TO RESIGNATION. HERE, YOU HAVE TO BE ABLE TO CONVICT A GUY BEFORE HE'S DEEMED UNFIT TO HOLD OFFICE. ─

THAT'S WHY AFTER 20 MONTHS OF INVESTIGATIONS, DOZENS OF CHARGES, TWO DEAD WITNESSES AND A REPORT THAT DIDN'T REALLY CLEAR HIS NAME, RAY DONOVAN IS *STILL* MY SECRETARY OF LABOR!

WELL DONE, RAY!

TWO CHEERS!

THIS IS A GREAT COUNTRY, RAY.

I KNOW, SIR, I KNOW.

GBTrudeau

FRIENDS, AS YOU KNOW, THE LAST 20 MONTHS HAVE BEEN A TERRIBLE ORDEAL FOR ME. BUT I THINK IT'S NOW TIME TO LET BYGONES BE BYGONES, EVEN THOUGH IT MEANS PUTTING DOZENS OF PERJURERS BACK ON THE STREETS.

IN THAT SPIRIT, I'VE ALSO DECIDED TO CALL OFF MY FORMER COMPANY'S INVESTIGATION OF THE SENATORS INVESTIGATING ME. I'M GIVING ORRIN HATCH AND THE REST OF THE COMMITTEE A CLEAN BILL OF HEALTH!

ABOUT THE AUTHOR

Garry Trudeau launched his Pulitzer Prize-winning cartoon strip, DOONESBURY, in 1970. When he took a leave of absence in December of 1982, the strip was appearing in 710 newspapers in the U.S. and abroad, with an estimated readership of 60 million. His animated film, "A Doonesbury Special," made with John and Faith Hubley for NBC-TV, was nominated for an Academy Award and received the special Jury Prize at the Cannes Film Festival. His characters have also hit Broadway, in the musical "Doonesbury."